Colour up to Christmas

A Colouring Book and Advent Calendar

Alison Brown

The Book Publishing Academy

***

© Mrs Alison J Brown 2017

***

ISBN -13: 978-1-912420-21-6

***

Details of other titles can be found at:

www.alisonbrown.info

Created with love
for my granddaughter
Suzie

Adam and Eve sinned against God and so...

God's beautiful Creation was spoiled.

Genesis 1, 2 & 3

Death and disease came into our world.

2

God said, 'One day I will send a Saviour!'

Genesis 3:14-15

Abel was very sorry for his sinful ways.

His lamb offering was accepted by God.

Genesis 4, Hebrews 11:4

Noah and his family also believed God.

4

They were safe in the Ark when God judged the sinful world!

Genesis 6, 7 & 8

God spoke to a man called Abraham.

He said, 'Follow me to a new land and I will bless you richly.'

Genesis 12

Abraham would have many descendants.

All the families of the earth would be blessed through him.

Genesis 12 & 15

Abraham and his wife Sarah were very old.

7

The birth of baby Isaac was a miracle!

Genesis 21

Isaac had twin sons.

8

Esau did not listen to God, but Jacob did.

Genesis 28

Jacob's son Joseph was a ruler in Egypt!

9

He kept God's people alive during a famine.

Genesis 37, 39-46

God's people lived in Egypt until they...

ended up in slavery.

Exodus 1

They were thankful for God's protection.

11

God called Moses to lead them safely out.

Exodus 2-14

In the wilderness God taught them how they should worship him...

and he gave them the Ten Commandments.

At last they came to the land that God had promised to Abraham.

13

Joshua led them now.

Deborah, Gideon and Samson led them too.

God kept his people safe for a reason.

Judges 4, 6-8 & 13-16

They would write the books of the Bible...

15

and bring the Saviour into the world!

But once they settled in the promised land...

16

they wanted a king instead of their God!

1 Samuel 8

They had Saul, David, Solomon and others...

17

Some kings were bad and some were good.

1 Samuel 10 - 2 Samuel 24, 1 Kings 1-11

God's people would not honour the Lord.

18

God sent prophets such as Elijah and Isaiah to warn them.

1 Kings 17, Isaiah 8

Fierce armies came from other places...

19

to fight God's people and ruin Jerusalem.

2 Kings 17 & 24-25

God's people were taken as prisoners!

20

They were sorry they had not obeyed God.

Psalm 137

Some of them were faithful to God...

21

such as Daniel, who really loved to pray!

Daniel 6

God showed mercy to his sinful people...

22

and let them return to rebuild their city.

Nehemiah 1-7

God's prophets had said the Saviour would come soon!

23

He would be born in Bethlehem of Judah.

Micah 5:1-2, Matthew 2:5-6

Angels sang in the sky to announce his birth!

24

The shepherds were the first to hear.

Luke 2:8-14

They found the baby sleeping in a manger.

25

He was Jesus, the sinless Son of God!

Luke 2:15-20, Matthew 1:21

The people rejoiced to see God's own Son!

26

Wise men from the East brought gifts.

Matthew 2:7-12

Jesus was a king so they gave him gold.

27

He would also be a priest so they gave him frankincense.

Luke 1:32, Hebrews 4:14

Jesus was the Lamb of God who was going to die...

28

so their third gift was myrrh.

John 1:29

He died at Calvary to pay for our sin, but he rose to life again!

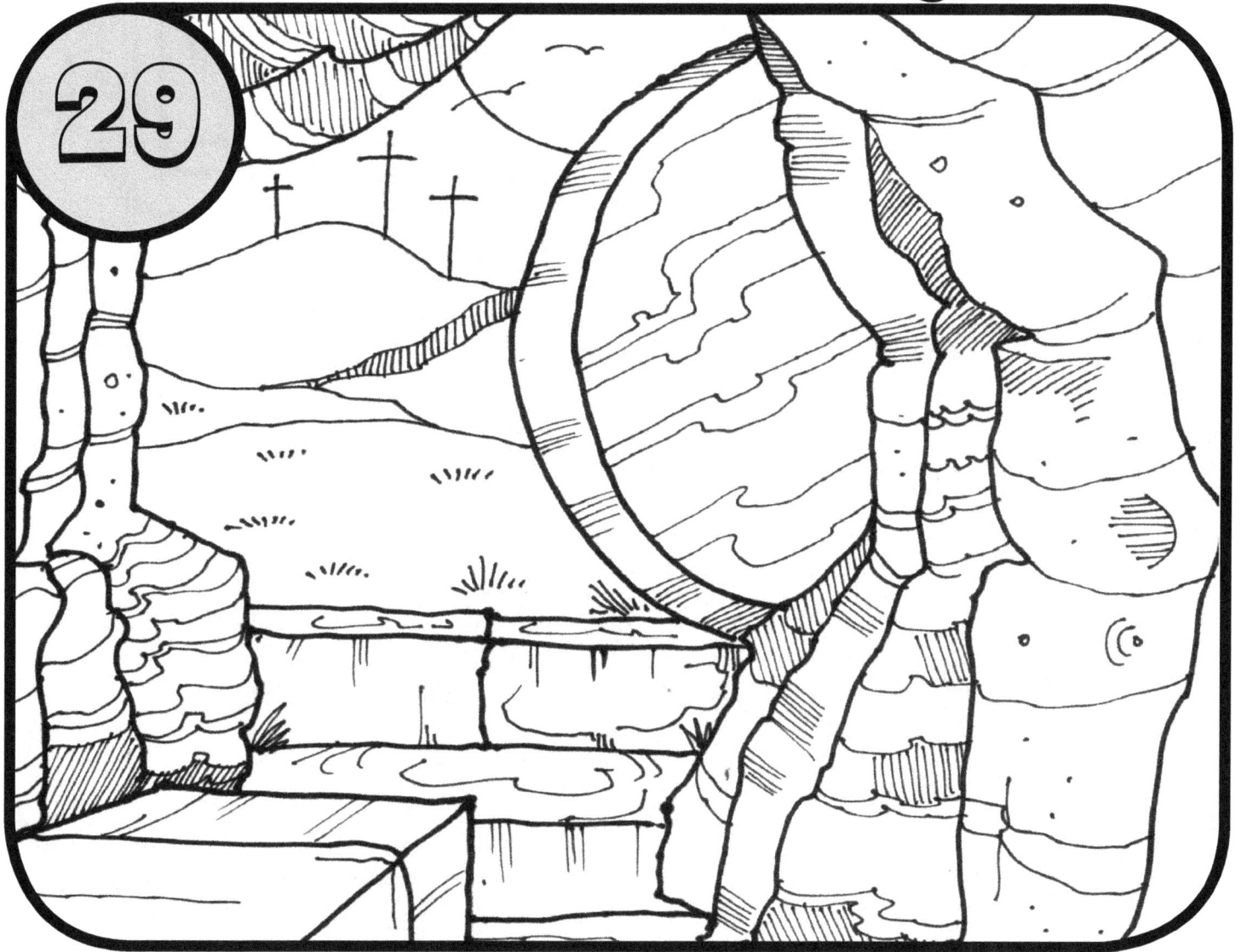

29

The Bible says Jesus is the door to heaven.

Luke 24:1-9, John 20:26-29, John 3:16

Jesus himself said, 'I am the way, the truth, and the life:

John Chapter 14

no man cometh unto the Father, but by me.'

(John 14:6)

www.ingramcontent.com/pod-product-compliance
Lightning Source LLC
Chambersburg PA
CBHW081234020426
42331CB00012B/3171